THE LAST READING OF CHARLOTTE CUSHMAN

By Carolyn Gage

ISBN: 978-1-716-13319-0

Praise for *The Last Reading of Charlotte Cushman:*

"A tour de force… Magnificent… beautifully crafted script"

—*Advertiser,* Adelaide, Australia.

"Electrifying… enormously entertaining, absorbing, and brutally honest… Anger, pride, frustration, flair, narcissism, nastiness, grandeur, passion, indomitable skill, jealousy, razor-edged revenge and ultimately heart…"

—*Sunday Mail,* Adelaide, Australia.

"Never have I heard such raves from so many of our festi-goers… clearly the highlight of the… National Women's Music Festival!"

—Mary Byrne, producer Nat'l Women's Music Festival, Bloomington, IN.

"… nearly flawless in its appeal and execution... [Gage's] Charlotte brought an appetite to the audience they didn't even know they had… the audience reluctantly left the theatre…"

—*The Slant*, Marin County, CA.

"… flawless… a smashing performance…"

—*We the People*, Sonoma County, CA.

"… unabashedly lesbian, unabashedly theatrical…"

—*The Maui News*, HI

THE LAST READING OF CHARLOTTE CUSHMAN

The Last Reading of Charlotte Cushman is a one-woman show about the greatest American actress of the nineteenth century. Charlotte Cushman, a large woman of masculine appearance, was very "out" about her lesbianism, cross-dressing to play men's roles and referring to her partner as "my wife."

The play opens with an announcement that the performance will be canceled, but Charlotte, outraged that such a decision has been made without consulting her, charges on to countermand the order. Cushman, struggling desperately against breast cancer, insists on performing—and, taking up the challenge of her condition, devotes the evening to the subject of death. Having played many roles which require dying, Charlotte regales the audience with moving—and sometimes hilarious—scenes from *Macbeth*, *Hamlet*, *Oliver Twist*, *A Midsummer Night's Dream*, *Henry VIII*, and the notoriously bad melodrama, *Guy Mannering*.

Interspersed with her monologues are anecdotes about other actors, her family, and about the romantic intrigues of the lesbian community of American émigrées who were living in Rome in the mid-1800's. This community included Harriet Hosmer and Emma Stebbins, both sculptors of international reputation.

One woman (plus one very brief, walk-on part)
90 minutes
Single set

Introduction to *The Last Reading of Charlotte Cushman*

The Last Reading of Charlotte Cushman is a play about the lesbian actress, Charlotte Cushman, who had been very, very famous and powerful in the nineteenth century. In my play, she is on her final tour, struggling against the cancer that will kill her.

Facing a diagnosis of permanent disability, I wanted to write about coming to terms with disease and mortality. I wanted to write about a woman who was saying good-bye to her life in the theatre.

The play was also an act of revenge against an industry that had treated lesbians and masculine woman like freaks and outcasts. Here was a fierce, fat, "bull dyke" who, notwithstanding, had been the greatest English-speaking actress on two continents in the nineteenth century! It was empowering to bring her to life, and, through her, to get in touch with my anger and contempt for the kind of colonized female roles that are the staple in mainstream theatre—roles that relegate women like myself to positions as stagehands or character actors.

The heroic performer who defies death to keep the curtain up is theatrical cliché, but I didn't mind exploiting it, because the real drama of the play lay not in the plot, but in the celebration of butch sexuality that was represented by Cushman. The real Cushman had been a major womanizer, right up to the last years of her life.

This was the Cushman I wanted to celebrate—the scoundrel, the roué. I wanted to show my audiences the special charisma of the swashbuckling butch. As

Cushman says in the play, “I have always maintained that only a woman can play Romeo with any credibility.” The challenge of this play was to write a fascinating, funny, tragic, charming, rollicking, rant-and-roar, tear-jerking evening of theatre based on this larger-than-life theatrical legend.

CAST OF CHARACTERS

STAGE MANAGER: A man or woman of any age.

CHARLOTTE CUSHMAN: A large woman, masculine in appearance, late 50's.

Scene

The scene for the reading is the actual theatre where the play is being produced.

Time

The present.

THE LAST READING OF CHARLOTTE CUSHMAN

ACT ONE

Lighting is set at pre-show levels. An antique table and chair are center stage. On the table is a pitcher of water with a glass, and next to them is a stack of old books with markers in them. An elegant vase with an arrangement of flowers graces the table. The STAGE MANAGER enters, uncomfortable to be addressing an audience.

STAGE MANAGER: Could I have your attention please? I've been asked to announce that the reading tonight has been cancelled. It seems that the performer is ill, and she won't be able to appear—

CHARLOTTE: *(From the wings.)* Just a minute! Just a minute! *(CHARLOTTE CUSHMAN enters. She is a tall, white-haired woman in her late fifties. She is masculine in appearance and comportment, and she wears her hair pulled back off her forehead. Her outfit is unorthodox, but it suits her well. She wears a man's tailored jacket and tie from the 1870's over a long, full skirt of dark color. CHARLOTTE is a proud woman, fiercely in control of her own destiny. Her life has been the theatre, and her relationship with her public has always taken precedence over her relationships with lovers or friends. She is dying, and she knows it. This will be her last stand, and she pulls all the stops. She enters, out of breath.)* What do you think you're doing?

STAGE MANAGER: *(Turning in surprise.)* Miss Cushman—

CHARLOTTE: Who told you to cancel my reading?

STAGE MANAGER: They said you had collapsed in the dressing room.

CHARLOTTE: *(Enraged.)* Yes, and I have expanded again. I want to know whose idea it was to cancel the reading.

STAGE MANAGER: It was Miss Stebbins, your… your…

CHARLOTTE: *(A challenge.)* My wife? *(Enraged, she turns toward the wings to confront Emma.)* Yes, well, Emma tends to overreact sometimes. *(To Emma.) Don't* you? *(To STAGE MANAGER.)* I'm sure Emma told you all about my cancer, didn't she? My *breast* cancer? *(To Emma.)* Yes. *(To STAGE MANAGER.)* And did Miss Stebbins tell you that it was my cancer that brought me out of retirement four years ago? And did Miss Stebbins tell you that in these four years of touring, I have performed hundreds of readings and plays? *(To Emma.)* No? *(To STAGE MANAGER.)* And did Miss Stebbins tell you that in all these years, I have never missed a single performance? *Never*? *(To Emma.)* No? *(To STAGE MANAGER.)* But, if you and Emma feel that it would be better for me not to go on, I will be happy to withdraw… *(Scooping up her books.)* … *after* I have collected my full fee, of course.

STAGE MANAGER: *(An agonizing pause, during which the STAGE MANAGER turns first to Emma and then back to CHARLOTTE.)* Miss Cushman, if you're willing to—

CHARLOTTE: *(Dropping the books.)* Thank you, I am. Now, if you'll just introduce me, I think we can get on with our evening. *(She hands her/him a card and turns her back.)*

STAGE MANAGER: *(Glancing in Emma's direction before reading the card.)* "Ladies and gentlemen, it is my privilege tonight to present the greatest English-speaking actress of two continents, a performer who has entertained for three presidents and the crowned heads of Europe, an American artist whose interpretations of Shakespeare's tragic heroines are legendary, and a leading lady for four decades..." *(With a flourish.)* ... Ladies and gentlemen—Miss Charlotte Cushman! *(The STAGE MANAGER exits, and the lights come up on the set. CHARLOTTE turns to acknowledge the applause. She is still stung by Emma's interference.)*

CHARLOTTE: Well... *(Picking up the books.)* I was preparing to read a little Tennyson for you... and a little Bobby Burns... and some of Mrs. Browning's poetry tonight, but since Miss Stebbins has taken it upon herself to select a theme for this evening—death—I am afraid that the readings I had prepared are no longer suited to the occasion. Well... *(Pushing the books to one side.)* I shall just have to improvise. Death... *(She crosses to the table and takes a drink of water.)* The first time I encountered death, I was twenty-three years old and in bed with a prostitute. *(Sitting, she turns to the audience.)* That got your attention, didn't it? *(Turning toward Emma in the wings.)* See what you've started? *(To audience.)* This is all Emma's fault. *(A long look at Emma before she turns back to the audience.)* So—where was I? Ah. In bed with a prostitute.

Well, I was twenty-three years old and living in New York. I was what they called a "walking lady," which is the actor who takes the roles too large for the chorus and too small for the leads. This was at the Park Theatre. And it was excellent training, too. Everything was repertory in those days, and during my three years as a "walking lady," I performed over a hundred and twenty different roles. But what does this have to do with a prostitute?

I'm getting to it. The Park Theatre was managed by one Stephen Price, and it is an understatement to say that Mr. Price and I did not get along. You see, Mr. Price resented any actor who was more handsome than himself. *(She laughs.)* He saw it as his personal mission in life to drive me out of the company, and in February of 1839, it looked as if he just might succeed.

The Park Theatre was going to produce *Oliver Twist*, and there is a part of a prostitute in the play, Nancy Sikes. Well, in my day, no actress with any kind of reputation would touch a role like that, and Stephen Price knew it. So, naturally, he assigned it to me. If I took the part, I would be professionally ruined, and if I refused, I would be fired. Yes, Mr. Price finally had me where he wanted me.

And to tell you the truth, I considered quitting. It was quite an insult to be cast as a prostitute, and of course, he had done it in front of the whole company. But I had seen too many talented women lose out to temperament in this game, and I was determined not to be outmaneuvered. If there was a way to play Nancy Sikes without damaging my reputation, I was going to find it. And I was equally determined to see Stephen Price hoist on his own… *(Pausing to consider.)*… *tiny* petard. *(Laughing, she rises.)* So I accepted the part—graciously. And then I took myself down to Five Points. That was the area just east of Broadway—the worst slum in New York. And I rented myself a room at Mother Hennessey's, which was the cheapest and dirtiest rooming house I could find. That was where the streetwalkers and the drunks stayed, when they could afford a roof for the night. And it was there, at Mother Hennessey's, that I began to study the role of Nancy Sikes.

During the day, I went out on the street and watched the old women pick through the garbage, and then I watched the young women pick through the old men. I watched their hands, their hips, their elbows, their mouths, their teeth, their eyebrows. I watched them flirt, I watched them joke, I watched them steal—I watched the things that no one else was watching. And at night, I went to the saloons, and I studied the women there. *(Smiling.)* And sometimes the women studied me. On the third night, a young prostitute came into the bar. She was very sick, shaking all over, and she asked for water. They gave her a glass of whiskey, and she got sick all over the floor. The men thought this was funny. *(A long pause.)*

I went to help her, and it turned out she didn't have any place to stay for the night, so I took her up to my room at Mother Hennessey's, I undressed her, I helped her to bed… *(Pausing.)* And then she died. *(She sits.)*

That's it. That's the story. No last words, no touching prayers, no anxious faces hovering over the bed, no final embrace. A convulsion and she died. That was it. *(Reflecting.)*

"... Out, out, brief candle!
Life's but a walking shadow, a poor player,
That struts and frets his hour upon the stage,
And then is heard no more. It is a tale
Told by an idiot, full of sound and fury,
Signifying nothing."

What did I do? I took her clothes. *(Rising with mock indifference.)* Of course, I took her clothes. I had a show to open, and they fit me… *(With anger.)* And then I went back to the Park Theatre, and I gave them Nancy Sikes. Oh, yes, I gave them Nancy Sikes. Not the whore with the heart of gold, not the feisty little spitfire from the wrong side of town—oh, no—I gave them a prostitute the likes of which they had never seen on a New York stage, even though they passed a dozen girls just like her on the way to the theatre—even though half the men would go home with one of these girls on their arm.

But I gave them a prostitute they could see, not just look at—but really see. I gave them a prostitute that made them weep the tears that no one shed that night at Mother Hennessey's. And weep they did. You see, real life is too painful for most people. That's why they come to the theatre.

So—would you like to see Nancy? You would? All right. This is from the third act, where the boy Oliver has been kidnapped by Nancy's pimp, Fagin. Her boyfriend, Bill, is threatening to turn his dog loose on Oliver, and Nancy is determined to stop him. Here's Bill… *(Turning away to get in character as Bill Sikes.)* "I'll teach the boy a lesson. The dog's outside the door—"

(As Nancy.) "Bill, no! He'll tear the boy to pieces."

(As Bill.) "Stand off from me or I'll split your skull against the wall!"

(As Nancy.) "I don't care for that, Bill. The child shan't be hurt by the dog unless you first kill me."

(As Bill.) "Shan't he? I'll soon do that if you don't keep off."

And here comes Fagin: *(As Fagin.)* "What's the matter here?"

(As Bill.) "The girl's gone mad."

(As Nancy.) "No, she hasn't."

(As Bill.) "Then keep quiet."

(As Nancy.) "No, I won't… Now, strike the boy, if you dare—any of you! Don't "dear" me! I won't stand by and see it done! You have got the boy, and what more would you have? Let him be then, or I will put that mark on you that will bring me to the gallows before my time! Oh, yes, I know who I am and what I am. I know all about it—well—well! God help me! And I wish I had been struck dead in the streets before I had lent a hand in bringing him to where he is. Ah, me! He's a thief from this night forth—and isn't that enough without any more cruelty? Civil words, Fagin? Do you deserve them from me? Who taught me to pilfer and to steal, when I was a child not half so old as this?—You! I have been in the trade and in your service twelve years since, and you know it well—you know you do! And, yes, it is my

living! and the cold, wet, dirty streets are my home! and you are the wretch who drove me to 'em long ago, and that'll keep me there until I die—" *(She lunges, as if to strike Fagin.)* Devil!"

(The gesture tears open CHARLOTTE's mastectomy scars, and she freezes in pain, her hand covering the place. Glancing toward the wings, CHARLOTTE holds up her hand to prevent Emma coming onto the stage.)

No! I'm all right, Emma. I'll be fine – *(Turning her attention toward the table.)* I just need a little water… and I'll be fine. *(Sitting, she concentrates on pouring the water. She gestures toward the wings, in order to divert attention from her condition.)* Emma. Emma Stebbins, my wife. *(CHARLOTTE forces a laugh.)* Emma and I have been together—what?—twenty years now? *(She looks toward the wings, in need of Emma's support.)* Nineteen? *(Relieved at Emma's response, she turns to the audience.)* Nineteen years. Emma's counting. Emma Stebbins, the world-renowned sculptor. We met in Rome. Emma was living with Harriet Hosmer – *(She turns toward the wings. Emma has apparently said something.)* What? Oh, it's all right. They don't care. *(To audience.)* Do you? I didn't think so. *(To Emma.)* See? They don't care. *(To audience.)* Emma was living with Harriet Hosmer. She is a sculptor, too. An excellent sculptor. Harriet Hosmer—Hatty. *(To Emma.)* May I tell them about Hatty? I know they want to hear about her. Everybody wants to hear about Hatty. May I? *(Emma has said something.)* What? *(Defensive.)* What about Rosalie? *(Pause.)* All right, I will… *after* I tell them about you and Hatty. *(To audience.)* Emma's a little touchy about Hatty.

Well—Hatty Hosmer. Hatty's not speaking to me now.

Something about our hunt club in Rome. Hatty didn't think it was fair that they never gave the tail—the fox tail—to the Americans. Of course, she's talking about herself. Hatty's always talking about herself. But I have to admit, she can ride the pantaloons off the Italians. But there was no need to blow the whole thing into an international incident, which is what she did. Well, apparently she felt I didn't give enough support to her cause. So now she's not speaking.

But it's not really about fox tails. It's about death. I know Hatty. She lost practically her whole family before she was twelve. Her mother died when Hatty was six, and then she lost her two brothers, and then her sister. I just don't think she can take anyone else dying on her. So, you see, she's decided to kill the friendship instead.

But you want to hear the scandal. Well, I met Hatty Hosmer in 1851. I was thirty-five, and she—bless her heart—was just twenty-one. And a cuter little tomboy you never saw. Oh, she was a wild thing! Reminded me of myself. Anyway, I was touring in Boston, and she had just come back from medical school. She had been taking anatomy courses for her sculpting. Of course, she was the only woman they let in the school. That was Hatty. *(Rising.)* Well, she came backstage to see me, and, frankly, she was quite smitten. And, to tell the truth, I was rather dashing in those days—prancing around in tunics and tights... I had good legs. Still do. *(She shows us.)* Anyway, Hatty started coming backstage after every performance—and bringing me flowers. *(She shakes her head at the memory.)* It was very sweet.

But I was married at the time—to Matilda Hays, and Matilda did not think it was so sweet. Matilda and I were having some problems. Oh, Matilda… *(She sits.)* She had shown up at my door in London—not unlike the way Hatty was showing up in Boston—asking me for acting lessons. It has always amazed me how many young women seem to be in need of my instruction.

Well, as luck would have it, I had just lost my touring partner, and I was in the market for a new Juliet for my Romeo. How's that for a line? *(Laughing.)* Worked, too. Matilda auditioned for me, and I cast her, and we became lovers on and off the stage. It was all very daring and very romantic, and we were so pleased with ourselves, we got married. That's right. We had a ceremony and exchanged vows of celibacy—referring to men, of course—and promised to be faithful for eternity. *(Laughing.)* And it *was* an eternity. *(Another burst of laughter.)*

It turned out that Matilda was not really up to the demands of a touring performer, and she retired from her public role as Juliet, but she continued to accompany me as my wife. She told me she was happy, and I believed her. I have never understood a woman who is actively miserable and not doing anything about it—but that was Matilda. And such was the state of our affairs when Hatty Hosmer knocked on my stage door in Boston. *(She is about to proceed with more confidences, when she sees Emma give her "the look." She assumes an air of wounded dignity.)* But there's no point in boring you with the details. One thing just led to another, and the next thing you know, Hatty was joining Matilda and myself in Rome that winter— *(To Emma.)* To study sculpting. *(To the audience.)* The whole thing was very innocent. *(Protesting to Emma, who has said something.)* It was! *(She starts to speak to the audience, but turns back to Emma.)* How would you know? You weren't even there! *(She rises, laughing. The joke has been on Emma.)*

Where was I? Rome… Yes, well, there had been one slight obstacle. Hatty's father, Hiram—but we all called him "Elizabeth." I can't remember now why we did that. *(Laughing.)* Well, anyway, "Elizabeth" was terrified at the thought of his daughter leaving him. I never met a more possessive man in my life. He had even built a little studio on the back of his house, just so that Hatty could stay home and be a little "sculptress." *(Soberly.)* Don't ever call Hatty a sculptress. *(She laughs.)*

Well, her father made us all promise that we would send Hatty back at the end of a year. That was twenty-five years ago, and Hatty is still in Rome. Well, Hiram had a fit and he cut off all the money. But Hatty had her revenge. Oh, yes, she had her revenge.

What she did was, she designed a monument in honor of a girl who had murdered her father—Beatrice Cenci. You don't know who that is, but, believe me, everybody in Rome knew about Beatrice Cenci. Her father had locked her up and raped and beaten her for years, and than she finally hired someone to murder him. Well, they arrested her, of course, and sentenced her to die—she was only seventeen—and the whole city was in an uproar, especially the women.

Well, Hatty's statue of Beatrice was something else. It was the most exquisitely beautiful female form I have ever seen—and I've seen a few. She has the girl lying on the stone slab of her prison cell, looking for all the world like an angel on a cloud—sleeping unmolested at last. And she has the sweetest little smile on her face. Hatty's statue of Beatrice has gone around the world now. Yes, it even went back to Boston, where Elizabeth could see it. Oh, yes, Hatty had the last word. She always does… She always does. *(Rallying.)* But the point of this whole story is how I met Emma. *(Turning toward the wings.)* You were hoping I'd forget. *(To audience.)* So, anyway, Matilda and Hatty and I moved to Rome. And then Hatty did what most young women do to older women who have helped them unstintingly and from the pure goodness of their hearts—she dumped me. And didn't Matilda just love that! Poor Matilda. She never could do anything on her own. She had to let Hatty use her in order to hurt me. So the two of them got together to act out their little melodrama for my benefit. *(Reflecting.)*

I have a horror of amateur theatricals, and so I booked a tour of England, leaving my little semi-retired Juliet to her understudy of a Romeo back in Italy. And, of course, after I left, there wasn't much point in the whole thing for Hatty, so she dumped Matilda. And then Matilda came running up to London, her little tail tucked between her legs, to see if I would take her back. I did, of course, but nothing could be the same between us—thanks to Hatty. But I had my revenge— *(Toward the wings.)* Didn't I? *(To audience.)* This is the good part.

Emma came over from the States to study sculpting, and of course, she met Hatty. Everybody who came to Rome had to see the Pope and Hatty. Not necessarily in that order. So, Emma met Hatty, and Hatty can be very persuasive when she wants to be. She talked Emma into living with her, and the next thing you know she was going all over Rome introducing Emma as her wife. Her wife! Hatty was about as domestic as her horse. But she made the fatal mistake of introducing Emma to me, and as Rosalind would say: *(Crossing seductively toward Emma.)*

No sooner met, but they look'd; no sooner look'd but they lov'd; no sooner lov'd but they sigh'd; no sooner sigh'd but they asked one another the reason; no sooner knew the reason but they sought the remedy.

That was twenty years ago – *(To Emma.)* Excuse me, Emma—nineteen… *(To audience)* And she is still with me.

Poor Hatty… But we're all friends now. Hatty even came and lived with us for six years. *(To Emma.)* Yes, we're all friends now… *(To audience.)* Except now, of course, with this death business.

Funny how everyone else is more upset about it than I am. They should know better. The only thing that kills an actor is a bad review. Audiences will forgive you if you die, but they will never forget a bad performance.

No, I have already died once in this lifetime, and once is enough, thank you. It was in New Orleans, the winter of 1835. I died every day for five months. Every single day. I'll never forget it. Nineteen years old, away from home for the first time—singing opera. You didn't know that, did you? Well, that's how I got started—and nearly how I got finished.

Yes, I was an opera singer. And I could have been a very good one, too, if my teacher hadn't insisted I sing soprano when it should have been obvious I was a natural contralto.

Well, the critics were brutal. Absolutely brutal. Would you like to hear what they said? Of course you would.

There are few things in this life which give us as much pleasure as other people's bad reviews. Well, let's see… "Seldom in tune, she possesses neither taste nor skill." You like that? Or "… we would as soon hear a peacock attempt the carols of a nightingale as to listen to her squalling caricature of singing…?"

Oh, I died a thousand deaths that winter. A thousand deaths. I had left Boston with such high hopes, and now it looked as if my life was over before it even started. I would go back to Boston, back to my mother's wretched little rooming house, back to a life of drudgery, back to Charlie Wiggins—the driveling little store clerk who was always pestering me to marry him. And wouldn't Mother have loved that! Yes, my life was over. *(As Wolsey.)*

> *"Farewell? a long farewell to all my greatness!*
> *This is the state of man: to-day he puts forth*
> *The tender leaves of hopes, to-morrow blossoms,*
> *And bears his blushing honours thick upon him;*
> *The third day comes a frost, a killing frost,*
> *And when he thinks, good easy man, full surely*
> *His greatness is a-ripening, nips his root,*
> *And then he falls, as I do. I have ventur'd,*
> *Like little wanton boys that swim on bladders,*
> *This many summers in a sea of glory,*
> *But far beyond my depth. My high-blown pride*
> *At length broke under me, and now has left me,*
> *Weary and old with service, to the mercy*
> *Of a rude stream, that must forever hide me."*

Cardinal Wolsey, *Henry VIII.* Charlotte Cushman, New Orleans.

But I never gave up. As long as I was still under

contract, I would perform—no matter how vicious the critics, no matter how rude the audiences, no matter how unkind my fellow performers. No, when that curtain went up, I was always in my place. Dying every second, but *in my place*.

Well, finally, one of the critics took pity on me. He suggested that I might be successful in a non-singing role. That was it. That was my break.

I took the notice to the manager of the company, and I begged him to give me a speaking part. Well, he didn't have much to lose, because I was still under contract for another month, and, heaven knows, my notices certainly couldn't be any worse. So he told me the role of Lady Macbeth was mine if I wanted it. I wanted it.

Lady Macbeth. In two weeks. Now, bear in mind I was still just nineteen years old, and I had never performed a play in my life—much less a Shakespearean play, much less a lead role. But this was it—my one chance, and *I could not fail*.

What did I do? I made a plan. I would impersonate a famous actor who had been a success in the role. Not a bad plan—except that the actor I chose was Sarah Siddons. Sarah Siddons. "The" Sarah Siddons. England's greatest tragedienne. Lovely Sarah Siddons. Petite Sarah Siddons. Charming, seductive, gracious, vivacious, flirtatious, *feminine* Sarah Siddons. *(She nods.)* Yes, Sarah Siddons… *(A damsel in distress, veddy proper accent.)*

> *Alack, I am afraid they have awak'd,*
> *And 'tis not done; th' attempt, and not the deed,*
> *Confounds us. Hark! I laid their daggers ready,*

He could not miss 'em. Had he not resembled
My father as he slept, I had done't.

(She laughs.) The director was concerned. He told me to be more passionate. *(Properly petulant.)*

... Go get some water,
And wash this filthy witness from your hand.
Why did you bring these daggers from the place?
They must lie there. Go carry them, and smear
The sleepy grooms with blood... "
Oh!

(CHARLOTTE gives a feminine cry of exasperation.)

... Infirm of purpose!
Give me the daggers!

(A long pause.) We were days from opening. The director was tearing his hair out. Finally he stopped the rehearsal. He told me I had no talent, that I was wasting my time, that I would never have a career on the stage, and that all my dreams were ridiculous.

Well, I might have accepted that I couldn't act. I might even have accepted that I didn't have a future—but that my dreams were ridiculous…? What did he know about the dreams of a nineteen-year old girl? What did he know about my wanting to hold another woman in my arms, to feel her soft breasts pressed against mine, to kiss her on the lips, to wake up in the morning with her head resting tenderly on my shoulder? What did he know about my dreams of having enough money so that the woman I loved could live with me for the rest of my life, so that I could travel anywhere I wanted, dress any way I pleased, do anything I liked with anyone I chose? Ridiculous? No, my dreams were not ridiculous. They were beautiful, and this man had no right to make fun of them.

What did I do? I reared up on my hind legs like a beast who has been cornered. I showed him my fangs, and I showed him my claws. I backed that poor fellow into a wall, my fists waving in his face, and I tore into him. I let him know exactly what I thought of his arrogance, of his conceit, and of his "Shakespe-ah." I don't know what all I said, but I know that I said it. And when I was all through, shaking from head to toe, tears running down my face, waiting for him to fire me—do you know what he did? He clapped. The son-of-a-bitch stood there and clapped. And then he said: *(Whispering.)*"Do it just like that." *(Smiling.)* And I did. *(She turns her back, for a moment to get into character. During this speech, CHARLOTTE directs rage toward her body and the disease which is ravaging it—alluding to the mastectomy at the end.)*

... The raven himself is hoarse
That croaks the fatal entrance of Duncan
Under my battlements. Come, you spirits
That tend on mortal thoughts, unsex me here,
(CHARLOTTE clutches her breast.)
And fill me from the crown to the toe top-full
Of direst cruelty! Make thick my blood,
Stop up th' access and passage to remorse,
That no compunctious visitings of nature
Shake my fell purpose, nor keep peace between
Th' effect and it! Come to my woman's breasts,
And take my milk for gall, you murth'ring
ministers,
Wherever in your sightless substances
You wait on nature's mischief! Come, thick
night,
And pall thee in the dunnest smoke of hell,
That my keen knife see not the wound it makes,

Nor heaven peep through the blanket of the dark
To cry, 'Hold, hold!'

(She collapses in the chair, out of breath and panting.) I stopped the show… Stopped it cold… *(Struggling for breath.)* They loved me... They loved me! *(Unable to rally, she signals toward the wings.)* I think this would be a good time… for us to take a break… *(Lights fade, as CHARLOTTE rises with extreme difficulty to exit. Blackout.)*

End of Act One

ACT TWO

Lights come up on the same set. CHARLOTTE enters. She has rallied during the intermission, and she paces the stage like an animal in a cage. Conscious that her time is running out, CHARLOTTE plays with a feverish energy bordering on delirium.

CHARLOTTE:

'Tis now the very witching time of night,
When churchyards yawn and hell itself breathes out
Contagion to this world. Now could I drink hot blood,
And do such bitter business as the day
Would quake to look on.

(Smiling.) Hamlet… Emma didn't think I'd make it back for the second half. *(To Emma.)* Did you? *(To audience.)* She didn't think I'd recover from my surgery either. I had a breast removed four years ago. One of the first operations of its kind ever performed… *(Pausing.)* A distinction which was not without disadvantages. *But*, I survived. *(To Emma.)* Didn't I? *(To audience.)* And here I am.

(Turning suddenly to Emma.) I'll tell you what, Emma—I'll make a bet with you. If I don't finish the show tonight, I'll cancel the rest of the tour and go home with you. How's that? *(To the audience.)* She likes that. *(To Emma.) But*, you have to agree, if I *do* finish the show, you will go with me to San Francisco. *(To the audience.)* I've always wanted to go there. They'd love me in San Francisco, don't you think? *(To Emma.)* Well, what do you say? Is it a deal? *(Rallying, she turns to the*

audience.) You are the witnesses! Miss Emma Stebbins has just agreed to accompany Miss Charlotte Cushman on a tour to California and points west.

(Turning toward Emma, who has apparently interrupted her.) What? *(Irritated.)* Of course, I'm going to tell them about Rosalie. I said I would, didn't I? *(To the audience.)* You want to hear about my first girlfriend, don't you?I thought so.

Rosalie… Rosalie Sully. I was twenty-six and she was twenty-two. Would you like to know how I seduced her? Well, I sat absolutely motionless for hours at a time and never said a word. You don't believe me? Her father was painting my portrait. *(She laughs.)* Rosalie Sully… *(Sitting.)* Well, Mother thought the whole thing was disgusting. She presented me with an ultimatum: Give up Rosalie or move out of the house… *(Defensive.)* What could I do? I was young, and I had no one to advise me. I did what I thought was the right thing. I felt I had no choice at the time… *(With mock contrition.)* I rented an apartment, so Rosie could sleep with me. *(Laughing heartily, she rises and crosses downstage.)* Oh, we were in love. We were so in love—and I had waited so long! Is there anything like that first girlfriend? It was sweet and tender and passionate and everything I had ever dreamed it would be. And more. And better. Rosalie Sully. My Rose. She died while I was over in England. Died at twenty-six… Beautiful Rose.

(Changing the subject abruptly.) But that reminds me—we were doing death this evening, weren't we? I suppose you want to see me die. That's what they pay me for. So—what's your pleasure? Suicide? Sword wound? Musket ball…? How about poison? Poison is

good.

This is Hamlet's mother, Gertrude. She has to die in front of both her husband and her son, but without upstaging either one of them. Needless to say, this is a role which presents a challenge for many women.

(CHARLOTTE, a vapid expression on her face, lifts the glass and sips from it as if it were wine. She suppresses a series of coughs, rises in alarm, only to lose her balance, and waves to Claudius to indicate that he is not to worry. Attempting to sit, she falls out of the chair and lies panting on the floor, but still indicates that there is nothing wrong. Pulling at the neck of her dress and gasping for air, she crawls painfully toward the front of the stage. She rejects an offer of help:)

No, no...
(Gesturing toward the table.)
... the drink, the drink—O my dear Hamlet—
The drink, the drink! I am pois'ned.
(A final suppressed gasp—and a wave to her husband to indicate that he is not to worry—and Gertrude expires.)

And then there's Queen Katharine. She dies of a broken heart. Henry the Eighth has divorced her, and this is her way of getting even. It takes her eight pages to die. *(Moving the chair center stage.)* I'll just hit the highlights. *(She positions herself by the chair.)*

My legs like loaden branches bow to th' earth,
Willing to leave their burthen...
(Snapping her fingers.)
... Reach a chair.
(She sits.)
So; now, methinks, I feel a little ease.

(She begins to sink, but rouses herself, irritably snapping her fingers.)

Patience —

(Coming out of character.) Patience is her maid. *(Katharine again, snapping again.)*

Patience, be near me still, and set me lower;
I have not long to trouble thee...

(Rousing herself and snapping her fingers.)

Cause the musicians play me that sad note
I nam'd my knell, whilst I sit meditating
On that celestial harmony I go to.

(She sinks, but, irritated, she rallies for another snap.)

... Bid the music leave,
They are harsh and heavy to me

(Coming out of character and rising.) Here's Patience: *(A long scream.)*

... How pale she looks,
And of an earthy cold... Mark her eyes!

(Another scream, and then she is Katharine again, rolling her eyes. She starts to die, but rallies.)

... Patience, is that letter
I caus'd you write yet sent away?...
... Sir, I most humbly pray you to deliver
This to my lord the King...
... Say his long trouble now is passing
Out of this world; tell him in death I blest him,
(For so I will.) Mine eyes grow dim. Farewell...

(Rallying.)

... Nay, Patience,
You must not leave me yet. I must to bed...

(She rises and falls back.)

Call in more women...
... Embalm me,
Then lay me forth. Although unqueen'd, yet like

A queen, and a daughter to a king, inter me.
("To hell with it.")
I can no more.
(Katharine dies, and CHARLOTTE rises to replace the chair.) Needless to say, Henry had the rest of his wives beheaded.

But you want to know about my most famous dying scene, don't you? It was in *Guy Mannering*. You've never heard of it, of course. One of those Sir Walter Scott potboilers.

I played Meg Merrilies, Queen of the Gypsies. And do you know my whole part was less than twenty minutes long—*and* at the end of the last act—and *still* this is the role everyone remembers? Not Lady Macbeth. Not Rosalind. Not Gertrude. No, Meg Merrilies, Queen of the Gypsies. It is one of the cruel ironies of the theatre, that an actress who has distinguished herself in some of the greatest classical roles in dramatic literature, can go down in history for twenty minutes of the worst applesauce ever written. Well, I have no intention of doing Meg Merrilies here tonight… *(She begins to thumb through one of the books.)* Still… she *did* sell out every performance… *(Still thumbing.)* And that was even during the war… *(More thumbing.)* Lines all the way around the block… *(Looking up suddenly.)* But you don't want to see it, do you? You do…? All right, but don't say I didn't warn you.

(She turns her back, musses up her hair, and whirls around with a wild leap. This speech is delivered with a thick Scottish burr. A critic of her day described this scene thus: "... she stood like one great withered tree, her arms stretched out, her white locks flying, her eyes

blazing under their shaggy brows. She was not like a creature of this world, but like some mad, majestic wanderer from the spirit-land.")

"The tree is withered now, never to be green again; and old Meg Merrilies will never sing blithe songs more. But I charge you… that you tell him not to forget Meg Merrilies, but to build up the old walls in the glen for her sake, and let those that live there be too good to fear the beings of another world; for if ever the dead come back among the living, I will be seen in that glen many a night after these crazed bones are whitened in the mouldering grave!"

(Jumping back to play the villain.) "Hark ye, Meg, we must speak plain to you! My friend Dirk Hatterick and I, have made up our minds about this youngster, and it signifies nothing talking, unless you have a mind to share his fate. You were as deep as we in the whole business."

(As Meg.) "'Tis false! You forced me to consent that you should hurry him away, kidnap him, plunder him; but to murder him was your own device! Yours! and it has thriven you well!"

(As the villain.) "The old hag has croaked nothing but evil bodings these twenty years; she has been a rock ahead to me all my life."

(As Meg.) "*I*, a rock ahead! The gallows is *your* rock ahead!"

(As the villain, pulling an imaginary gun.)"Gallows! You hag of Satan, the hemp is not sown that shall hang

me."

(As Meg.) "It is sown and it is grown, and hackled and twisted—"

(She is indicating a noose, when suddenly she makes the sound of a pistol shot and clutches her heart. A critic of her day has described her death in these words: "When Hatterick's fatal bullet entered her body, and she came staggering down the stage, her terrible shriek, so wild and piercing, so full of agony and yet of the triumph she had given her life to gain, told the whole story of her love and revenge." She screams and staggers downstage.)

"I knew it would be like this!" *(Collapsing on the floor, she crawls the entire length of the stage to snatch victory from the jaws of defeat. She speaks her dying words to Dirk.)* "It has ended as it ought."

(After dying a lugubrious death, CHARLOTTE rises and dusts herself off.) Meg Merrilies, Queen of the Gypsies… But I didn't just play queens. I played princes and kings, too. Breeches parts. That's what they called it when we took the men's roles. And why shouldn't we? They had all the lines.

I played Aladdin, and Oberon—King of the Fairies… And two cardinals—Richelieu and Cardinal Wolsey. I was the first woman to play Cardinal Wolsey. And, of course, Hamlet. I borrowed Edwin Booth's costume. *(Remembering.)* Filled it out better than he did, too. *(She laughs.)* But my most famous breeches part was Romeo. Oh, Romeo! How I loved to play that boy! Mad, passionate, tempestuous Romeo. I loved him! I *was* Romeo! *(Shaking her head.)* All those years of pent-up passion for my girlfriends… All those long nights of fantasy—and frustration! I felt as if I had been rehearsing for Romeo all my life.

And Susan was my first Juliet. My baby sister Susan. You didn't know that, did you? Yes, my sister and I acted together for ten years. And those were the best years of my life. Especially, *Romeo and Juliet*, and especially when we took the play to London. Yes, Susan and I were a team. Top billing: "Charlotte Cushman and her sister."

Well, Mother had a fit. It was bad enough that *I* was in the theatre, but Susan! Oh, no, not Susan! —not her precious, little, blue-eyed, baby girl! No, Mother had it all planned out that her *beautiful* daughter was going to marry a rich man, and that he was going to support the whole family, and then she and Susan would never have to work again. *(A bitter laugh.)*And Mother was in such a hurry to spare Susan a life of drudgery, she forced her into marriage at the age of thirteen. Thirteen. How did she get Susan to go along with it? Well, she told her that the man was sick and going to die soon—which is what he had told Mother—and that the whole thing was just a legal formality so that Susan could inherit his property. Well, needless to say, the scoundrel was lying about the state of his finances— *and* his health! One year later, there was Susan, my baby sister, fourteen-year-old Susan—pregnant, abandoned, and being hounded by an army of creditors. Well, I came to the rescue, of course. I was already supporting Mother and both my brothers.

But I'll tell you something— the day—the very *day* that baby was weaned, I marched Susan down to the Park Theatre and got her an audition. My baby sister was *never* going to have to depend on a man again—not if I could help it!

Well, they cast her, and then Susan and I started working together. You know, the women didn't usually team up—but *we* did. We knew each other's timing, we knew each other's business—There was no one in the theatre who could beat us! And we played everything—*everything*: Mistress Page and Mistress Ford in *Merry Wives*, Gertrude and Ophelia in *Hamlet*, Oberon and Helena in *Midsummer Night's Dream*, Lydia Languish and Lucy in *The Rivals,* Desdemona and Emilia in *Othello*, Lady Macbeth and Lady Macduff, and then—our most daring—*Romeo and Juliet*!

In 1846 we took the show to London. Oh, that was a story! But first we thought it would be a good idea to try it out in Scotland. Well, we managed to scandalize the entire population of Edinburgh. For weeks rumors were flying that Susan was an unwed mother, and that I was… well, what I am!

Of course, none of this would hurt our reputations in London. No, what almost stopped us there was a dead actor. That's right, a dead actor. His name was David Garrick.

It seems that Mr. Garrick had taken it upon himself to improve on Shakespeare's plays—which meant, of course, writing longer scenes for himself and cutting the women's lines. Oh, do I know David Garrick! He may have died before I was born, but I know him. I have been sharing the stage now for forty years with the David Garricks of this world, and they are no different now than they were a hundred years ago.

Well, Mr. Garrick had done such an excellent job of

promoting himself, that his version of *Romeo and Juliet* had become more popular than Shakespeare's. When Susan and I got to London to rehearse with the company at the Haymarket, there was not a single actor who knew the original version. Furthermore, they absolutely refused to learn it. No, they were not about to let two Americans teach them their Shakespeare—much less two women, much less a woman who intended to dress like a man and make love to her sister! *(Laughing.)* Well, Susan and I had no intention of performing the Garrick butchery—so there we were, on the verge of an actors' strike. Then, at the eleventh hour, the manager of the Haymarket stepped in. He posted a modest notice in the Green Room, to the effect that any actor who was not willing to cooperate with the Misses Cushman would be free to seek employment elsewhere.

And so we opened. December thirtieth, 1846. And we were an immediate sensation. I have always maintained that only a woman can play Romeo with any credibility. The male actors with the maturity and experience to handle the role are obviously too old to be boys. On the other hand, an experienced actress can impersonate a young man well into her forties—provided, of course, she has the right "attitude." *(To Emma.)* Then, too, there are those things that only a woman can know about what pleases a woman. *(To the audience.)* Apparently the critics agreed. They wrote that I put their gender to shame with my lovemaking. Yes, rumor had it that "Miss Cushman was a very dangerous young man." *(Laughing.)* So, Susan and I were a sensation. We ran for eighty consecutive performances at the Haymarket—which was a record. And then we went on tour to the provinces. And then Susan had to go and ruin it all. She got married… again! *(CHARLOTTE begins to pace.)* Helena, *Midsummer Night's Dream.*

Injurious Hermia, most ungrateful maid!
Have you conspir'd, have you with these
contriv'd
To bait me with this foul derision?
Is all the counsel that we two have shar'd,
The sisters' vows, the hours that we have spent,
When we have chid the hasty-footed time
For parting us—O, is all forgot?
All school-days friendship,childhood innocence?
We, Hermia, like two artificial gods,
Have with our needles created both one flower,
Both on one sampler, sitting on one cushion,
Both warbling of one song, both in one key;
As if our hands, our sides, voices, and minds
Had been incorporate. So we grew together,
Like a double cherry, seeming parted,
But yet an union in partition,
Two lovely berries molded on one stem;
So, with two seeming bodies, but one heart…
(With sudden fury.)
… And will you rent our ancient love asunder,
To join with men in scorning your poor friend?
It is not friendly, 'tis not maidenly.
Our sex, as well as I, may chide you for it,
Though I alone do feel the injury.

Yes, Susan got married. She got married and gave up acting. Or I should say, she gave up the stage. Her whole marriage was a performance, if you ask me. We were never close again after that. *(Agitated by her memories.)* Yes, Susan betrayed me. Just like Matilda. Just like Hatty. Just like all the women I have tried to love—they always leave me. I don't understand it. I have never abandoned a woman in my life. *(Turning with irritation toward Emma who has interrupted her.)* What? *(In a threatening tone.)* What about Rosalie? *(Pause.)* I told them she died. *(Bullying the audience.)* Didn't I? I told you she died while I was in England, didn't I? *(To Emma.)* See? I told them… *(She starts to address the audiences, but turns back to Emma with sudden ferocity.)* But you want me to say I murdered her, don't you? Stuck a knife in her heart like Iago—don't you? That I betrayed her, because I told her I would only be gone for six months, and instead, I stayed in England for three years.

(With rising anger.) Yes, I did stay. Because for the first time in my life I was a leading lady. For the first time in my life the managers were coming to *me.* And for the first time in my life, money—*real* money—was finally coming in. And wasn't that the whole point? To make enough money so that Rosie and I could live together for the rest of our lives? Yes, I stayed, and I would do it again.

(To Emma.) But you want me to say that I killed her. *(To audience.)* Do you know that Rosalie wrote to me every single day of those three years? Every single day—and sometimes twice a day! What was I supposed to do with all those letters? Drop everything to answer them? Was I supposed to apologize to her, because my life was full of excitement and glamour, while she had nothing better to do than clean her father's paintbrushes—and write me those interminable letters? Was that my fault? Was I supposed to give up my life and live hers, because she couldn't live mine? *(Enraged, she turns toward Emma.)* Is that what I was supposed to do? If Rosie killed herself, it wasn't my fault!

(Turning back to the audience with manic intensity.)

So—would you like to see some of my Romeo? Let's see… This is the scene at the end of the play where Romeo is entering the vault of Juliet's tomb. He thinks she has died, but she is really just asleep—and he is going there to kill himself.
(She attacks the scene with Romeo's frenzied desperation.)

Give me the light. Upon thy life I charge thee,
What e'er thou hearest or seest, stand all aloof,
And do not interrupt me in my course.
Why I descend into this bed of death
Is partly to behold my lady's face,
But chiefly to take thence from her dead finger
A precious ring—a ring that I must use
In dear employment—therefore hence be gone.
But if thou, jealous, dost return to pry
In what I farther shall intend to do,
By heaven, I will tear thee joint by joint,
And strew this hungry churchyard with thy limbs.
The time and my intents are savage-wild,
More fierce and more inexorable far
Than empty tigers or the roaring sea...

(Turning suddenly, she confronts the body of Juliet. Exhausted, CHARLOTTE drives herself to finish the monologue.)

... O my love, my wife,
Death, that hath suck'd the honey of thy breath,
Hath had no power yet upon thy beauty:
Thou art not conquer'd, beauty's ensign yet
Is crimson in thy lips and in thy cheeks,
And death's pale flag is not advanced there...
... Ah, dear Juliet,
Why art thou yet so fair? Shall I believe
That unsubstantial Death is amorous,
And that the lean abhorred monster keeps

Thee here in dark to be his paramour?
For fear of that, I still will stay with thee,
And never from this palace of dim night
Depart again. Here…
(She falters.)
… here will I remain
With worms that are thy chambermaids; O,
here…
(She falters again.)
Will I set up my everlasting rest,
And shake the yoke of inauspicious stars
From this world-wearied flesh…
(She has difficulty going on.)
… Eyes, look your last!
Arms…
(Faltering.)
Arms, take your last embrace!

*(As she reaches out her arms for Juliet, she breaks down and turns her back to the audience. Racked with sobs, she collapses in the chair, her face in her hands.)*I'm sorry. I can't finish it. *(She takes out a handkerchief, breaks down again, and then collects herself.)* I'm sorry… his has never happened before. I… was just... remembering Rosalie.

(Taking another moment.) Yes, I did betray Rosie. There was another woman. Of course there was another woman. I was only thirty, and I was the toast of London. Of course there was another woman. I know Rosalie heard the rumors. Mother would have told her. (*Weary, but without bitterness.)* Yes, Mother would have enjoyed that.

And Rosie began writing me desperate letters. And I

wrote angry letters back, denying everything. So then, of course, she knew. The truth was, I had outgrown Rosalie. How could I tell her that? But I never should have lied to her. That was the betrayal. Rosie deserved the truth. We all deserve the truth.

(Looking at Emma.) Well, Emma… it looks like you've won the bet. *(She begins to gather the books.)* You know, the great tragedy of *Romeo and Juliet* is that Romeo doesn't know that Juliet is still alive. He puts himself through all that agony for nothing. All the time Juliet is just waiting for him… waiting for him, and he doesn't have the sense to know it.

(A long look at Emma.) Well— *(She rises. This is her farewell to forty years in the theatre.)*

Our revels now are ended. These our actors
(As foretold you) were all spirits, and
Are melted into air, into thin air,
And, like the baseless fabric of this vision,
The cloud-capp'd tow'rs, the gorgeous palaces,
The solemn temples, the great globe itself,
Yea, all which it inherit, shall dissolve,
And like this insubstantial pageant faded
Leave not a rack behind. We are such stuff
As dreams are made on; and our little life…
(Pausing to smile.)
… Is rounded with a sleep.

(To Emma.) Let's go home, Emma. I'm tired. *(To the audience.)* Goodnight. *(Exiting with tremendous dignity. Blackout.)*

End of Play

www.ingramcontent.com/pod-product-compliance
Ingram Content Group UK Ltd.
Pitfield, Milton Keynes, MK11 3LW, UK
UKHW020137250726
13967UKWH00002B/709

9 781716 133190